I0486887

Credit Card Debt 109: Options and Answers

Mark Beimfohr

ISBN-10: 1439216878
ISBN-13: 978-1439216873

Updated January 2024

Preface

This book is about my personal battle with Credit Card Debt, what I did.

I would like to apologize beforehand for all of the she/he's, him/hers, and theys. I dealt with real people with real names, but I did not think it was necessary in this book to reveal who I dealt with or what their gender was. I also didn't disclose what credit card companies I dealt with.

Know that you are not alone in your battle with credit card debt, or any debt.

I first published this book in 2008. The first several pages tell that story. I ran into credit card debt trouble again, unfortunately, in 2022/ 23. I added that story to this current book. I took two different routes to solving my credit card debt, so this book now shows options.

My hope is that I can help other people work through their credit card debt perhaps a little easier than I did.

Table of Contents

Convenient Privilege or Evil Necessity

Credit Cards – those wallet sized plastic cards that are a part of the American lifestyle nearly as much as apple pie and baseball. Just swipe the card at your local retailers' checkout station to purchase anything from children's diapers or school supplies to your vehicles wax or tires, to your homes remodeling needs or even the family groceries. And with the World Wide Web we can use them to purchase birthday presents, graduation gifts, or even sit in your chair while Christmas shopping; Hanukkah if you prefer, or whatever; and any other special occasion. The point is we can shop online using our credit cards without having to leave our homes.

Pay your balance in full when the bill arrives at the end of the month, and you have just borrowed money for free. Everything is good - everyone is happy. Pay a portion of the balance and you have just borrowed money (your remaining balance) at a relatively high (sometimes very high) rate of interest.

Miss a monthly payment and you will pay a late fee along with your monthly rate of interest. Miss a couple of payments and your interest may even increase. The late fees and interest collected on the balance of your account are two of the ways credit card companies make their money.

Convenience Checks – those paper checks that credit card banks may send us through the mail so that we may use them as we choose. Many come with a low, limited introductory interest rate so that we may cash these checks and pay off higher interest credit cards; basically, borrowing from Peter to pay Paul. These checks usually have a fee associated with them when you cash the check (usually based on the amount of the check) and of course you will usually pay at least some interest on the amount of the check if you do not pay the balance the next time your bill arrives. And, if you do not pay the balance before the introductory interest rate expires you will pay a higher interest rate for the remainder of that loan you made on your credit card by cashing the convenience check.

We all know how the system works. I'm just refreshing your memory and trying to make a point on how convenient and easy it is not only using that credit card and/or convenience check you have in your possession, but also how quickly and easy it is to fall behind on paying your balance in full each month. Credit cards are quick, they are convenient, and because of shopping over the internet they are many times necessary. It is only when we spend a little too much on ourselves or others; or we become dependent on the cash we can get from the paper credit card checks. Then perhaps we fall behind on our payments - and that is when it can all become evil and very stressful.

How I Got There – My Story of Debt

       Americans are raised with the idea to work hard and pay their debt. When we attend a party or other gathering one of the first things that we ask when we meet a new person is 'what do you do'? Ironically, the person whom we ask that question knows exactly what we mean – they do not say, what do I do 'when'. They know immediately that we are inquiring about what they do for a living. And if the question is asked of us, we also know that the subject is about our job –what we 'do'.

       Although no one asks about debt it is basically assumed that we have it. If a neighbor or family member buys a car, sends a son or daughter to college, or buys a large television; the talk is often about how they can afford it. Debt, too, is very much a part of life as an American. Our savings accounts dwindle as our debt accumulates.

       Running up credit card balances can and does happen with the occurrence of various circumstances. We may use our credit card or their checks to help us through the loss of a job, an illness in the family, or trying to put our kids through school. Current issues may cause us to lean on our credit cards as the mortgage mess, buying gasoline; or maybe it's just financial mistakes that we have made. Many forms – same result – the credit card balance becomes too large to handle, we struggle to make the minimum payments, and unfortunately the minimum payment barely takes care of any of the actual balance we are trying to pay off.

I became disgruntled with my job back in the late 1990's. I felt like a monkey could do the job I performed every day. I felt I wasn't really using my brain and had feelings that I was not very useful – that life should be more fulfilling. So, at age thirty-nine, I decided to go back to school; at first part-time at a local Junior College and after two years I went on to a university. I still worked, at least part-time, as the University was only about fifty-five minutes from where I lived. However, debt did begin to accumulate.

I studied Architecture at the University and was working toward a Bachelor of Science in Architectural

Studies Degree. But, in architecture, you have to have a master's Degree from an accredited University before you can actually take the test and earn a license to be an Architect. So, after graduating with a bachelor's in science degree I put in several applications to attend a university that offered a master's degree in architecture. One of my instructors that taught design classes at the University urged me to put in an application to his alma mater which was the University of Utah at Salt Lake City. I liked this teacher, and it was cool when in mid 2002 I received an acceptance letter from the University of Utah's Architecture Department. Now this would be very exciting for a nineteen-year-old without home-ties, ready to go see and explore the world! But for me, a forty-something year old, living with his girlfriend and five children between us; it was exciting but also very scary.

During the summer of 2002 I researched loan possibilities and basically found nothing. The local banks that I was acquainted with were not interested in giving me a loan and letting me wait to pay it off until after I graduated. I had a little money saved but not enough. Then my dad gave me a loan with an agreement that I did not have to begin paying it off until after I found a job. The loan was not large enough to cover the entire two years I would be in Utah but at least it got me started.

I mentioned my family a little earlier. My girlfriend and I became engaged during my two years of study in Salt Lake City, and we have a yours, mine, and ours family. I have two daughters from a previous marriage, she has a son and daughter from her previous marriage, and we have a daughter together. They are all adults now but when I was attending the University of Utah, they were fairly young. It was very difficult for me to be away at school, and it was hard for them while I was gone. In August of '02 I packed the truck full of some furniture, a bed, a computer, and headed off to Salt Lake City. It was a very sad good-bye, and I actually did not plan on returning back home to Illinois until the semester break in December. Well, it was even tougher being away than I had imagined so two weeks later, on Labor Day Weekend, I flew back home. It was awesome to be home and spend time with my family. I ended up flying home quite a bit. The airlines were still recovering from 9/11 so the flights were fairly inexpensive, and the plane was hardly ever crowded. I remember one flight back to Salt Lake City when there were only about ten passengers on the entire plane. Also, the three-hour flights allowed me to study both on my way home and back to school.

When I left for the University of Utah in Salt Lake City I had every intention of working, at least part-time. I figured I could be a waiter, or cashier somewhere, some sort of a job to earn cash. I had located an apartment within walking distance of the University, so I didn't have to use much gas while I was there, although gas was not such an issue then anyway. But there were the other bills: monthly rent, utilities, food, school supplies, and out-of-state tuition was quite high. Not to mention the fact that my fiancé was back at home in Illinois, with the kids, trying to make ends meet there. So, we had two homes and all the bills that went with them.

It did not take me long to realize I was not going to be able to work and earn a master's degree, school was too hard. I would get up in the morning, walk to school, remain at school till around 9:pm or so, and walk back home to do more studying. The second (and final) year I had one computer at school and one at the apartment. I do not think I could have made it through without both computers. My weekends were spent getting up and doing schoolwork on the computer until it was time to go to bed – I am not kidding it was that hard and that much work. Some of the kids did work and attend school but I do not know how they did it, maybe if I had been younger! I did, however, work during the month I was home for semester break, and I did work the summer in between school years. Out of the twenty-two months I attended school I worked in only four of them. So yes, I relied on my credit cards to help me make it financially through my schooling at Salt Lake City.

   After graduating from the University of Utah in May of 2004 I came home and began looking for employment. I was hired in my field of study toward the end of June in the same year. That fall my fiancé went back to school to earn her degree in accounting (we certainly could not both attend school at the same time). Earning her degree took three semesters, a year and a half, and during that time she only worked part time. So again, all of our credit cards suffered a little bit more. Upon graduating she too landed a job in her field of study, and she enjoys her work.

So, that is enough about me and my family. The next few chapters will tell of information that may help you make decisions about your credit card debt. I simply wanted you to know that you are NOT alone. Credit card debt is not something that any of us plan, it can happen slowly or quickly – before we know it, wow – the balance or balances are out of hand. We are not stupid. We are not dead beats. I read an article recently about credit card debt and the author called people who are late or have stopped payments with their credit card accounts – dead beats. That author knows nothing about the circumstances that caused the late payments or the stopped payments. She or he should walk in other's shoes before he or she begins the name calling. We are all people. I made the charges; I cashed the checks – I did want to pay the balance.

Selling My Assets

This is a short and kind of sad chapter - but an 'important' one for you. As I mentioned before we Americans are raised with the idea of working hard and paying our bills. 'Not' paying our debts is very taboo – it is just not done. And filing for bankruptcy as a result of our debt seems to be one of the most shameful things we can do.

With that eating at me I sold several thousand dollars worth of assets trying to do anything I could to keep up with my credit card payments. In hindsight it was a mistake. I sold the assets in hopes that things would get better, that somehow before the cash from selling my assets ran out, I would be in a better position to pay the credit card balances. Another thing we are taught as Americans is to be hopeful. Unfortunately, I was to the point of fooling myself, it is better to be a realist and admit you are in trouble.

In early 2006 I sold over $15,000.00 worth of personal stock that I owned – stock that I bought when I sold a house a few years back. That money is all gone now; pretty well all of it went to the credit card companies. In early 2007 I sold my retirement account of the company I worked for before I went back to school. This amount was almost $12,000.00 and it too is now gone. The majority of this went to the credit card companies as well.

In mid-2007 I paid off a high interest credit card using some of the limited low interest convenience checks I talked about earlier; basically, borrowing from Peter to pay Paul. Then I received a letter from that credit card company stating that I could no longer use the credit card I had just paid off. They kept the account, I could see it on their website when I visited my account, I just could not use it. They stated something about my debt to earnings ratio or something to that effect – I don't remember exactly. Anyway, the point is that even though at that time I was not behind on a payment to that credit card company or any debt that I had; they took the privilege of using that card away. By stating this I wanted you to know that you may not always be able to count on using your credit cards to keep you afloat. They are owned by the bank, and they can suspend or end your charging privileges even if you are current with your account. I was already treading water, so I knew when the bank did this to my credit card that I was going to be in trouble fairly soon.

In August of 2007 I sold my 1908 Victrola that was beautiful and had been in my family for over fifty years. For those of you that know antiques it was the 'Lions Head' Victrola, it played both metal discs (records I always called them) and 33 1/3 rpm records. It was in its original condition and yes it was in working order. I hated to sell it. I kept a couple of my favorite records in hopes that someday I can play them again.

So, there you have it; almost thirty-five thousand dollars worth of my assets sold trying to keep up with my credit card bills. And yes, the majority of that money went directly to the credit card companies. The sad thing is I wasn't really any better off than I was before I started selling assets. The balances do not reflect that I paid them that money because about all I was able to pay was the minimum monthly payments. In a chapter to come I will tell you how much my monthly payments were and the interest rate I was being charged. This chapter is really about you recognizing that if you have to sell your assets to make your credit card payments it is time you do something more drastic. Do not hang on to the false dream that things are going to get better because they probably will not.

During my dealings with the credit card companies, and other companies and organizations, they all have asked if I had any assets I could sell. My response was that I have already sold almost all of them – a sad reality.

Options I Researched

This is another important chapter for you. I'll tell you about some of the legwork I did and about the options I discovered.

There are several commercials on the radio each day advertising debt settlement companies. They promise to have you out of debt in no time while negotiating your debt in half, or less than half. These commercials finally got the better of me (I sit in my office working most days with the radio on) and in early 2007 I contacted one of them through his/her e-mail. I knew my debt was getting worse and farther along however, I did not want to talk to anyone about it. We e-mailed back and forth several times and she/he was giving me the details of that company's program. Most of these companies' ads on the radio say that your debt to the credit card companies has to be at least ten thousand dollars (I made that criterion easily). The company I e-mailed told me in order to participate with them you had to have a good reason for the debt to have risen that high; and they said my reason of going back to school and not working was a good reason. I would imagine that those companies do not turn many people away so I am guessing that you have a good reason and would be eligible as well. The lady/man I was e-mailing told me that if someone enrolls in their program with around twenty thousand dollars in credit card debt then the monthly payments would roughly be three hundred dollars a month for forty months. If you do the math that total is twelve thousand dollars, which is sixty percent of the original twenty thousand. He/she said a good debt settlement company can settle your debt for fifty-five to sixty-five cents per one dollar, and that also includes all fees. After talking to that company, a little bit more in May of that same year I never contacted them again. I don't know why but that option just did not seem the way for me to go. I had heard that debt settlement (paying the credit card companies' 'part' of your debt and they write-off the remainder) gives you a bad mark on your credit score. This bad mark, I believed, stayed on your credit report for seven years. (I later found out that staying on your credit report for seven years is not true.)

Another option that I found on the internet was a company claiming they could teach me the negotiation skills needed to deal with credit card companies. That I could negotiate my debt down by perhaps fifty percent myself and not pay the debt settlement companies fees. That if I paid them about four hundred dollars for their book, they would tell me when the right time to negotiate was and how to get the best settlement. I did not go this route because I did not have the four hundred dollars and I figured if I was going to talk to the credit card companies myself then I would just try and learn it myself as I went along.

While we are on the subject of books; online bookstores and your neighborhood bookstores have several books on debt and credit card debt and several other money related topics. I did explore this and looked at several books that seemed to be pretty good. Several of the people that write these books are money experts, I am not. I am someone who lived through it and is telling you about my experience. It certainly doesn't hurt to read some expert advice. Read the reviews that are posted online when you click on a book that interests you.

The reviews will tell you a general idea of what the book is about and if the people writing the reviews liked the book. Then you can decide if you want to purchase a book.

A Credit Counseling Company was another option I explored. The one I called was recommended by a credit card company (I'll talk more about that recommendation in the next chapter). I am sure, as with about everything these days, that you need to be careful of which money management company you choose. Most are probably good companies but there are always the few who will not have your best interests in mind. Reputable companies will work with the credit card companies and negotiate a lower interest rate so you can make a payment and actually be paying on your principle. With the company I dealt with their representative went over my finances on the phone. They wanted to know what my income was and how much my expenses totaled. After about six weeks they sent me a personal debt management program. It was a packet that included all the financial information that we went over on the phone, my current credit card balances, their proposed monthly payment for me to make, and the estimated payoff dates of those credit cards. They want their client to sign a debt management agreement which shows how much you agree to pay them each month so that they can make payments to your credit card debtors. They also add a twenty dollar per month fee, which they keep, but I thought that was fairly reasonable. They negotiated my payments from about $2600.00 per month that I was paying the credit card companies to just under $1300.00 per month. So, they were cutting my payments in half, and I would be paid up in about five years.

You can see from the numbers that this company did a pretty good job; they cut my monthly payments in half. This may be the way for you to go. I would suggest that you at least talk to them and see exactly what they can negotiate for you. And I think working with a Credit Counseling Company is a good way to go if you are concerned about hurting your credit score. You may be able to work with them without even missing a payment on your credit card bill(s). Your credit card company can recommend a good credit counseling company because they would not want to deal with a company that was not reputable. This option also keeps the credit card companies happy for awhile. Whenever they called, I simply told them I was working with a debt management company, and they would be satisfied with that – short and not too stressful phone calls. I did, however, decide not to sign up with this company because I felt I was at the point that I could not even afford the thirteen hundred dollar a month payment. I was hoping I could negotiate a better repayment plan with the credit card companies and at this point was not concerned about my credit score.

I am sure there are several more options out there that you can think of that I did not. One I did consider was a loan from my bank, but I didn't think they would loan me the money and spread the payments out far enough so that I could afford them. I encourage you to look into all your options. Then do some research of your own and you may decide that one of them may sound right for you. Just be careful as I am sure there are companies out there that are perhaps not one hundred percent legitimate. And some may prey on vulnerable and confused consumers with out-of-hand credit card debt. They know how stressful that debt is and may promise you false hope just to get some of your money themselves. So, make sure you understand all the facts of their programs before you send them a check.

I chose the option to deal with credit card companies themselves. I will tell you about the experiences I had dealing with them in the next chapter.

The Credit Card Companies

Dealing with the credit card companies directly is how I chose to handle my credit card debt problems. Yes, I heard the horror stories about the constant phone calls and the pressure that their phone specialists put on consumers to scare them into paying their bills. But I figured since they were the one I owed the money to then they should be the companies I deal with. I wanted us to try and figure out this problem together, whether it was some sort of settlement or a repayment plan.

I owed two credit card companies a substantial amount of money. I'm not going to name those companies. They are large well-known companies and that's all that matters for this book. By early December of 2007 the cash that I had received from selling the Victrola back in August was pretty well gone just trying to keep up with the high monthly credit card payments. After we did our Christmas shopping for five kids and the rest of our family and friends it was gone. There was no way I could make the $2600.00 in monthly payments to those credit card companies, so that December I did not pay them anything. I knew it was time for me to do something drastic and this was the best way I could show them that I could not continue in the direction in which I was going. I am not suggesting that you do this, and I did not like it. We are raised to pay our bills, but that is what I had to do.

I had been a credit card holder for one of the companies since 1997. I was not too happy with them ever since they suspended my use of their credit card I told you about previously. That card had about a twenty-five-thousand-dollar limit and if they had not suspended that card, I felt I could still be manipulating debt and not be in the trouble I was in. But I realize now that this is just borrowing from Peter to pay Paul. If they had not suspended that card, I would have kept going and hoping that my credit situation would get better until that card was maxed out too. I had two accounts with them that carried a balance, one that I would consider large and the other fairly small. The cards had a total balance of a little over $21,000.00 when I missed my first payments. One was due toward the end of December of 2007, the other due the first week of January 2008.

I was beginning to cringe at work whenever the phone rang as the cards fell farther behind in their payments, I knew a call had to be coming. From the research that I had done I read that the person to talk to when you want to negotiate your debts is called a debt negotiator – simple enough. I really did not know what I would say to the banks when they called but I thought perhaps I would ask for their debt negotiator. The day finally came and when I picked up the phone I could hardly talk – I felt so badly, so ashamed, I really just wanted to cry. It was horrible! The man on the phone was simply asking why I was over ten days late. Still, I could not answer him. He asked if it was just an oversight on my part, if I had just forgotten. I finally heard myself mumble in a weak voice that I needed to talk to a debt negotiator. The man did not answer me, he just hung-up. That is when I decided I would call the banks; that waiting around for them to call me was not the thing to do. Maybe we could work something out and that talking to them would not be so bad. But I knew that as badly as I felt this would not be easy either.

With another company I had been a credit card holder since 1996. I have three accounts with them that carry a balance, one that I would consider quite large and the other fairly large. The third credit card I had with them was a gas card which can be used for normal charges, but I use it almost entirely to pay for gasoline. I will just be referring to the two cards with high balances. The cards had a total balance of a little over $35,000.00 when I missed my first payments; one was due in mid December, the other toward the end of December 2007. So, on the four accounts I owed the banks over $56,000.00 – a lot of money.

I called this company in January of 2008. They had sent me a letter reminding me that I was late with a payment, and they included a 'special needs' number if I needed help. I called that number and the person that answered the phone transferred me to a specialist. The 'specialist' told me that I was not late enough for them to worry about and then he/she recommended a credit counseling company that they cooperate with and gave me their number. Not Late Enough?! Well later in this chapter I will tell you when they evidently DID think I was late enough to worry about. Later that afternoon I called the credit counseling company and that is the company I told you about in chapter four. They were very nice people. The counselor went over my finances on the phone (it takes about thirty minutes) and said I would be receiving a packet with my personal debt management program information in the mail.

As I mentioned in the last chapter it takes about six weeks for them to send you the packet, so it was about mid-March of '08 before I received mine. As I also discussed in chapter four, talking to the debt management people gives you something to talk about to the credit card companies when they call. They are very satisfied with their clients working with a debt management company like that – and that is all you have to tell them and swiftly they are off the phone. During that time both credit card companies called me about once a week to once every ten days, so it was not all that bad. All of their phone specialists had been very kind and courteous; none of them threatening or trying to make me feel ashamed for not paying them. All the rumors one hears about the terrible harassment that you receive from the credit card companies were not true, at least it wasn't for me - not up to this point.

I will have to say that I had become used to telling the card companies that I was waiting to see what the credit management people would offer. Even after I received my packet and felt that I could not afford their payments, I still told the card companies for about a week or so that I was waiting to hear from the debt management company. Toward the end of March'08 one of the credit card companies called. Their representative told me that my accounts were coming up on ninety days late and that it would just get worse from there. She/he was actually talking about my credit score getting worse. After ninety days you receive a bad mark on your credit report that lowers your score. I was not concerned about that, I really just wanted to take care of these large debts no matter how long it took. But if keeping your credit score as high as possible is a concern of yours then you must work out your debt before it turns ninety days past due; I guess. Their representative explained to me that they had programs to help their customers pay back the debt. I was busy at work that day and I told him/her that I would call them back later in the week.

I called them back after about a week. I talked to the same person from a few days ago and that representative told me that their programs were probably better than the debt management companies. She/he offered to put the two accounts together and put me on a five-year repayment plan at a four percent interest rate which would amount to around a $450.00 payment per month. He/she also said that they could settle the debt if I paid $8,000.00, perhaps even $7,000.00, but they would have to get it approved. So that's around thirty-three percent of what I owed them, but I did not really want to do that. Their representative told me that at one hundred sixty to one hundred eighty days late they would charge off the debt so I should be deciding what I wanted to do. I called the other credit card company after that. Their representative offered me some type of five-year plan, but I must not have thought it was very good because I did not write it down (sorry). However, they did tell me about a short-term program that they had in which I would pay a little over $400.00 per month for twelve months. Then they could put me on a longer-term program after the twelve months was finished. This person explained to me that at one hundred sixty to one hundred eighty days past due they would probably sell my accounts to a collection agency so I should decide on what to do before that.

I called the companies from my office after regular working hours and everyone else had gone home. After I talked to them, I took my calendar down and turned it to the month of May. I wrote in May to have something done about this credit card debt by the end of the month. At the end of May, the debts will be one hundred fifty days late, and I was hoping these issues would not go past that.

Towards the beginning of April, a representative from one of the companies called me and told me about their Balance Liquidation Program. This person said they would consolidate my two account debts into one, wave several fees that have accumulated since December, and give me five years to pay them back at a 4 percent interest rate. That would have a repayment plan of about $625.00 per month – he/she said that they would write off the debts at seven months if I did not do something by then. A few days later the other card's representative called me. This person offered me a five-year program in which the large debt would have a seven percent interest rate and the smaller account an interest rate of twelve percent. This computes to about $495.00 per month but, if you look at the last paragraph, that offer is worse than the last one I received. I got off the phone with that representative and it was not five minutes later they called me back with a different offer. This time he/she offered me a seventy-eight month pay back program. They would wave some fees that have accumulated since December, give me a zero percent interest rate on the large account, and a four-point five percent rate on the smaller account. These totals compute to about $315.00 per month for seventy-eight months.

Not too terrible bad. But I was holding out hoping that they would offer me a plan that would lower my monthly payments even lower. I was willing to sacrifice a zero percent interest program if they could just offer a longer-term plan that would lower my monthly payments. These repayment plans by the two credit card companies were plans that they offered to me. I do not know if they offer everyone the same plans, but I would guess that they would at least be similar. I am sure they would have some type of plan for you too.

After my accounts became over one hundred days late the phone calls from the two companies increased quite a bit. They were each calling me at least once a week after that and some of the people were not quite as nice as before. Sometimes I would receive calls from one company a couple of days in a row. And they would tell me that I have not spoken to any of their representatives in over a week. I would say, 'yes I have' but I could tell they did not believe me.

One day on my way home from work they called, and I talked for a while to their representative. About five minutes after I hung up my cell phone rang again; it was them again. I explained to them that I just went over all of this and their representative then said that I had not talked to one of their people in more than a week. They became a little snotty, so I went ahead and talked to them a little bit too. I do understand that they need to call, however they need to keep better records so that they actually know when they did call.

I would sit at my desk at work and when the phone rang, I would cringe and hope it was not for me. Many times, I would just turn my cell phone off. It becomes a very stressful ordeal and starts to consume you. There were many days that my credit card debt was the first thing I thought about when I awoke and the last thing I would think about when I went to bed. It is hard on you and becomes hard on your family as well. I mentioned in chapter two that I am engaged, and we have five kids between us. When you are stressed with this type of credit card debt you don't have much inside yourself to give to anyone else. The kids never knew about all of this, but they did know something was wrong. When they asked, I would just say that money problems are getting to me. They all have enough problems of their own without worrying about mine. They knew back then we had money problems, and it stressed the kids out enough. They did not need to know just how bad it really was. My fiancé knew of course, she was very supportive, even when I became short with her. I want you to know that if you do not want a large increase of stress in your life then you should make a deal with the credit card companies before your account becomes one hundred days late.

In early May of '08 I received a letter from a collection agency letting me know that one of my larger accounts had been referred to them for collection. Well then, at about one hundred twenty days late I guess that company DID think I was late enough to worry about! I was surprised to receive this letter because all the phone employees that I had talked to told me their company would not do anything with the debt until it became one hundred and sixty days late. I guess upper management had other ideas. It was even more surprising because this debt was the only one they handed over to the collection company; maybe because it was the larger of the two accounts. It was not the account that was past due the farthest. This loan payment was past due since the end of December and the smaller of the accounts was late since mid-December, so it was barely one hundred twenty days late. Anyway, this is a good thing for you to know – do not always believe what the phone representatives are telling you. I am sure they are explaining to you what they think is factual but someone higher-up with the company may decide something different.

The collection agency representative called me about mid-May – she/he was not a people person. He/she tried to make me feel bad and tried to pressure me into giving them money to pay this past due account. Yes, it is his/her job (and she/he liked it), but there are better ways to deal with people. The other phone representatives I mentioned that were not always nice were perhaps just having a bad day. Think about what their job is every day. I am sure they come across some people that were not nice to them and they may take it out on the next person they call. But this person from this debt collection agency – he/she enjoyed not being nice.

Their representative told me I needed to pay $4,097.00 to bring the account up to date. I explained that I could not do that, so she/he suggested paying them $853.00 to bring the account up for the month. Well, I did not see how that was going to help because I would be back in the same situation in thirty days. This representative told me that I had to have the money because I had not paid the credit card company since last November. He/ She suggested that I was basically hoarding the money instead of paying them each month. Well don't I Wish!! I tried to explain to this person that the only way I was able to keep the payments up the last few years was by selling assets. He/She just kind of laughed and I knew they did not believe me – unbelievable. The representative offered a cash settlement of $15,000.00 but I explained there was no way I could come up with that kind of money. The representative then told me that he/she would just tell them that I was refusing to pay the money. I was not refusing to pay them any money. I told her/him I would be happy to work out a monthly repayment plan that I could afford. But that was not good enough.

May was now halfway over and I would look at my calendar at work and see the note I wrote back in March to have these issues settled by the end of May. The phone calls from the two credit card companies and now the collection agency was more frequent and very stressful so on May 19th I decided to pay a little money on all four of the accounts. One hundred fifty days late was coming quickly and I did not want the accounts to be just written off as bad debts. I received some money back from my '07 taxes and so I had some cash in the bank. I estimated I could afford to pay them about $450.00 so I figured up some percentages to see how much I could pay each account. One credit card company got two hundred eighty dollars total and the other got one hundred seventy. I knew this wasn't much, but I hoped that if they saw at least a small payment maybe we could work something out that I could afford.

Shortly after that one of the credit card companies called and offered me an 80-month program. They said the large account would be at zero percent interest for a term of eighty months which made the payments around $290.00 per month. She/He said the smaller account would be for seventy-three months and also zero percent interest and those payments would be around twenty dollars per month. This representative told me that the accounts were getting close to one hundred fifty days late and that I did not want that to happen. He/ She said that you get a mark-five on your credit report when the payments become one hundred fifty days past due (I think it was mark-five, it was something like that). Anyway, they said the account would leave his/her desk and then there may be no more deals offered. I told them I would call them back soon.

A representative from the other company called about a day after that and offered me a program for the small account that repays the debt in five years. He/She said the program would have a two percent interest rate and the payment would be about $259.00 per month. I asked her/him if that applied to the larger account as well (the account with collection agency) and they said yes, they could set that one up at two percent for five years as well. I told them I would be calling them back soon too.

A representative from the collection agency called the same day. (busy day for credit card debt collection). I told him/her that I had just talked to a representative from the credit card company, and I was setting up a repayment plan with them. She/He told me that I would not be setting up a payment plan with them, and I could hear the person clicking on the computer in the background. They were looking at my account and said something about a code being on the account – I knew right then that I should not have told this representative about the credit card people calling me.

I called one of the credit card companies a few days later and we set up the eighty-month, zero percent program. We set up automatic payment dates for the first six months and he/she said my accounts would show up as current on my credit report before then. They even had me cancel the payment I had set up last week. They said I could just use that $170.00 as part of my first payment. So, my repayment plan for this company was around $310.00 per month. I will say one thing – when I got off the phone with their representative it was like a weight was lifted off my shoulders. Some of the stress was gone, at least for now.

I called the other credit card company that same day. We set up the sixty-month, two percent interest program on the smaller account and my payments are around $259.00 per month. They set up automatic payment dates for the first five months and said too that the account would show up as current on my credit report before the five months were passed. I asked if we could set up the larger account and they said - no. Even so, by setting up one of the accounts for repayment I felt another weight was lifted. A little more stress gone, at least for now.

A representative from the collection agency called me toward the end of May and asked what the credit card people had said about a repayment plan. I told her/him that they told me they could not do that because it was being handled by someone else. He/she told me that was because the credit card company 'did not want' this account put on a payment plan. They again offered me a settlement amount of $15,000.00 and again I said I did not have that kind of money. The representative told me she/he would be in the office till four o'clock central time and that I could call him/her back by then. Well, it was hard for me to believe the credit card company did not want this account on a repayment plan. But then again, they did turn it over to a collection agency at only one hundred twenty days late, so who knows.

Instead of calling the collection agency before four I decided to call the credit card people back one more time after four. I called them from my office, again after working hours, and I told the representative that the company handling my debt would not work with me. That person brought up my account on their computer and asked if someone had talked to me today about my debt, that there was activity on my account from today. I told them that it was the person from the collection agency and then they said that they must be affiliated with the credit card company or there would not be activity on my account. Made sense to me. That representative told me to stay on the line and they would see if they could contact a collection agency representative – and they did. Well then, the collection agency told me they could put me on a short term or long-term repayment program. He/She said that I should call back shortly because the person I needed to talk to was at dinner. Why did the other person, the one I had been talking to, not mention anything at all about a repayment plan?

I called the collection agency about 6:15 pm and she/he told me about the five-year repayment plan and a twelve-month plan that has lower payments. I asked if it was possible to be on the twelve-month plan first and after that go to the five-year plan and they said yes. He/She said I had to make a good-faith payment to the credit card company (two percent of the account balance) and that she/he had to get the short-term payment plan accepted. I told him/her to go ahead and try to get the short-term plan accepted.

In early June the collection agency finally called me back. Their representative told me that they would not approve the short-term plan. However, I was approved for the five-year plan which had a two percent interest rate with payments of $456.00 per month. He/she said that since I was on the five-year payment plan with the smaller balance then this account was to be put on the five-year repayment plan as well. This was disappointing as I was really hoping to save $100. to $150.00 per month by being accepted into the short-term payment plan first. This is another example of the managers at the credit card company making different decisions than what the phone specialists said could be done. I realize the phone representative explained to me that the short-term plan had to be approved, it was not guaranteed. But the other credit card company's phone specialists had to have programs approved too; the difference is the managers at that company approved them. The collection agency representative said that if I did not accept this plan then the entire amount of the account would be due. That meant phone calls again, possibly worse, and I did not want to deal with that stress. So, I accepted the five-year plan and we set up some automatic payments as with the other accounts.

Around mid-June a collection agency representative called me and said the credit card company was not taking off any interest as they said they would. The representative wanted to have a conference call with us all on Thursday morning. When they called me, they could not get his/her phone to accept a conference call. They had the credit card company on one phone line with me on the other but could not put us together. The representative said she/he would talk to them and then call me back, and he/she did. I asked why they even needed me on the conference call, and she/he said it was because the credit card company was going to offer me a better deal than the $456.00 per month and I needed to be on the phone to accept the agreement. This made me excited. The collection agency said they offered a 60-month plan with me paying $365.00 per month and my account would be shown as current after a few payments–wow! They said the credit card company said they would wave some fees and forgive a little of my debt and that she/he could go ahead and set it up if I agreed, and I did. So, after making two payments of $456.00 I would then pay $365.00 per month on the large debt for the remainder of the five years – cool.

There you have it. I am sorry about all the numbers which may have confused you. Basically, I would be paying back one credit card company $310.00 per month for eighty months. The other, I would be paying $624.00 a month for five years. I will be paying about thirty-six percent of what I was paying, and it will almost all be going toward the principal. All of my accounts would be marked as current after a few payments and my credit score can then start on its way back up. I hoped I could afford these payments because I did not want to go through anything like this again!

Important Stuff

You need to remember that I am NOT a financial expert. This is just my story of my credit card debt, and I am passing it along to you in hopes that my experience will help you. I made some mistakes along the way, and I hope that you will learn from these mistakes. Perhaps then dealing with your debt will not be as stressful for you. Also keep in mind that the credit card companies may handle your situation differently, for better or worse, than they did for me. Research all the options I talked about and that you can think of before you do anything drastic. And if you think you might need to talk to a lawyer that handles financial situations then perhaps that would be a good choice for you.

Remember too that you are NOT alone. There are many of us struggling with credit card debt, and all kinds of debt – it is part of most of our lives. I know that you probably feel isolated and alone but take to heart that you are not. There are good options out there to help you. Also know that there are people in this world that may want to take advantage of you. The credit card companies' phone representatives would many times ask if I was dealing with a debt settlement company. They told me that several of their customers were, and it was a nightmare for them. They would pay the company money and their debt was not being taken care of. Of course, the credit card companies would not like debt settlement companies because they want all of their money, but I doubt they train their phone specialists to ask about it and just say that. The company I dealt with did seem legitimate to me and their representative was always helpful and nice but be careful. Usually if something sounds too good to be true it is, do not believe all of the promises you hear!

An important fact I learned during this experience that I can pass along to you is that stress becomes almost unbearable. You may be thinking, "Well it already is" and I do realize that but be prepared because it is likely going to get worse. The shear volume of phone calls alone is enough to make you scream, especially if you fall behind more than one hundred days. You just have to somehow grin and bear it. I remember talking to a phone specialist from one of the companies, I do not remember which, but anyway we laughed about something or another. The phone representative said, "At least you still have your sense of humor" and it is important that you keep that. Carrying debt is better than someone you love having poor health or even worse, death. I have read before about a person that had over ten thousand dollars of credit card debt and committed suicide because of it. Please do not do that! You have people that love you and if you are feeling like ending your life, please seek help and talk to someone. If you are someone that does not deal with stress very well then please work out your situation as quickly as possible.

Another thing to remember, if you are to the point where you have to sell assets to keep up with your credit card payments then you need help. STOP hoping that things may get better and take your debt into your own hands. You will know ahead of time if you are in trouble so the time for action is then and there. Do not procrastinate, sell assets, or try to hang on, hoping for better days. If I had not sold about $35,000.00 in assets just so I could keep paying high interest monthly payments on my accounts, I could have used that money to pay down the balance after I negotiated.

It made me a little torn between – yes, I made those charges and want to pay my bills and – yes, I was paying a combined interest rate of around 25% plus I sold many assets; so both credit card companies already received the money I borrowed from them! I was paying a combined total of $1080.98 per month on interest charges alone! Learn from my mistakes and do not squander assets.

One consequence you may encounter while you are going through this battle of credit card debt is that your other credit card companies may cancel you, even if you are not using them. I had a different company cancel two accounts that I had with them. I had been their card holder customer since 1995 and I was not late with any payments to them. I did not even have a balance at that time – but I was canceled. Another also canceled a credit card I had with them, but they said it was because of inactivity – yea ok, whatever. I would suggest you keep a small balance on all your credit cards before you do something drastic and keep most of them up to date. Our modern, go-fast world pretty well makes credit cards a necessity, so you at least need one.

The last chapter may run together for you so I will bring up a couple of interesting points about those negotiations. In early April of 08 One credit card company offered me a seventy-eight-month repayment program with a zero percent interest rate for the large account and a four percent rate for the smaller one. The payments would have been about $315.00 per month. I accepted their offer in May which has payments of about $310.00 per month. Both accounts have a zero percent interest rate with the smaller one having a term of seventy-three months and the larger account a term of eighty months. The difference as you can see is five dollars a month. Not much gained for all the phone calls I endured for those extra days. Waiting another month just puts on more interest and fees.

Also, in April of '08 the other credit card company offered me a five-year repayment plan in which they would take-away several fees and set the interest rate at four percent. This made the amount of my payments about $625.00 a month. They transferred one of my accounts to a collection agency less than one month later. I ended up agreeing on a five-year repayment plan in June with a two percent interest rate on both accounts which has combined payments of $624.00 per month. This is $1.00 less per month than the offer they made in April, and I had to add-on the good faith payment of over $500.00. Thus, waiting with them was actually worse than settling earlier.

So, if you get to one hundred days late with your payments take a close look at the deal they offer you. It may be about as good an offer as you are going to get. And trust me; the phone calls do get worse after those one hundred days.

The Financial Crisis

I first published this book towards the end of 2008. I was working in the construction industry and was laid off in December of that year. With the financial crisis of '07 and '08 came pretty well the end of construction projects in my area. I was out of work for about two years. I did receive unemployment compensation and found part time jobs but not enough to pay what I had negotiated with the two credit card companies. How about that for not-so-great luck? After going through all that I had to do it again.

I'm not going to go over all of that as I have put you through enough. I was able to save a little money between the negotiations and being laid off so that helped. I ended up settling with both companies for lump sums. They knew I wasn't working and actually gave me a break. I paid them a portion of what I owed them, and they forgave the rest. Maybe it turned out not to be the worst luck, but I sure didn't feel lucky being laid off for almost two years.

Present Day Troubles

During 2022 because of business decisions and some investing decisions that didn't work out as I hoped. I was beginning to lean on some of my credit cards again. And again, always thinking, better financial days are coming, I just need to use them a bit more to keep afloat. I'm not going to go over all of that either. We all have our financial hardships and stories of why we got in trouble with too much credit card debt, or any debt. By the end of 2023 I was in trouble, I had to do something. What I did is different than what I did before so that is why I am adding to this book. It will tell you about another option.

I needed help so I started looking for answers. I waited too long to negotiate with the credit card companies themselves and I was not going to sell assets this time. Pretty well all through 2023 I was paying over $1,600.00 a month to three credit card companies: just spinning my wheels. I paid over $19,000.00 to them in 2023 and got nowhere. I paid them more than I had charged because of very high interest rates and fees. I knew I could not continue.

January of 2024, I applied for a personal loan through Discover Financial Services, I think that's what they are called anyway. I figured if I could borrow from them to pay off the three high credit card balances, I would be ok. Even though they were charging over 17% interest, and the loan would be for six years. But they said no.

The very next day I was searching the internet for another option, maybe a loan with a different company. This day and age it is even worse than it was 15 years ago, so you have to be careful who is honest and who is not. I found a company that is on the Forbes list of best debt relief companies for 2024 and has great ratings with the Better Business Bureau. I don't know if I should add that companies name or not, but I will say the company name begins with an 'A'. I went to their site and started typing in my information. Name, address, phone number – and then I stopped and ex'd out of their site. Not really knowing if this was the right answer. Just a few minutes later they called me, I didn't answer. I smoked a couple of cigarettes out in the garage just stressing and thinking – and called them back.

Their phone representative agent was very friendly and helpful. They wanted to know how the credit card balances go so high. Not a detailed explanation, I think they just want to know if life caused the balances to increase or from being careless. They were not willing to give me an unsecured personal loan either, but they did have a debt relief program. With that, I would stop paying those three credit card companies and they would negotiate my debt to zero. I pay a bi-monthly fee to them, a little over $500.00 a month for 52 months. Less than a third of what I was paying to the three credit card companies and less time than a personal loan. They work with a lawyer firm that specializes in negotiating with credit card companies. I said yes. They did tell me that small local banks sometimes will not work with them. I don't know about that as I have always dealt with the national credit card banks.

They said to stop paying your credit card companies immediately, as I did when I negotiated with them directly several years ago. Credit card companies will not work with you if you continue to pay them. They told me credit score companies look at individual records toward the middle or end of the month and will adjust ones score up or down at the beginning or middle of the next month. I remembered how some credit card companies cancelled my card several years ago even when I was not using them. So, I went grocery shopping and used those cards to give them a balance. It is difficult to navigate in this world today without at least some kind of credit card.

When you stop paying your credit cards and begin negotiating; either directly or through a company, your credit score will take a hit. So, if you are planning on making a big purchase such as a house or vehicle you may want to wait to deal with the credit card companies after that. The good news is that it does not take seven years for your credit score to recover. As soon as your credit card debts are taken care of your credit score will begin to improve. I recommend getting a new, low maximum balance credit card. Use it and pay it off at the end of each billing cycle. This will help improve your credit score faster. I was pleasantly surprised back in

'08/ '09 how quickly it went back up.
I'm hoping that happens again this time,
and I think it will.

I do not know what the future
brings or how this will all work out. But
I can tell you I feel better stress wise and
feel more financial hope since I decided
to do something about my credit card
debt. I think you will too. And I did
learn that credit card companies still will
negotiate down the debts as they did
back in 2008. So, this book has given
you a couple of different ways to go.

If you are reading this book, it is
probably time for you to act. Don't wait.

I thank you for buying this book.
I hope it helps you and lets you know
you are not alone.

Why 1 0 9

This chapter has nothing to do with credit card debt, or any kind of debt, but you may find it amusing as to why the 1 0 9 is in the title of this book. I am over 60 years old and this number 1 0 9 has haunted me ever since I can remember.

I wish I had a dollar for all the times I glance at a clock and see the numbers 1:09. Of course, my imagination runs away with me, and I start thinking about the bad things that are going to happen to me in January about every year - 1/09. So far so good, Ha-ha. Back when I could afford to buy stock, I actually bought a stock with the ticker symbol – OZN. Because if you put number-words to the letters it becomes: One, Zero, Nine. Of course, that stock didn't make any money. Even when I was attending school at the University of Utah I would glance at the clock and - 1:09 both am and pm. A little strange and still happens today. I also have played 'pick three' lottery using the number 109. Never even came close to winning so I stopped.

Anyway, I thought perhaps if I put the numbers in the title of this book it would help people remember the book (You know, it's the one that has a 109 in the title).

I talked about values that we learn while growing up in America. I certainly do not mean that other countries have no values. Or that their citizens are raised with the notion that they do not have to pay their bills. The United States is what I know, I have lived here all my life. I am guessing that several other countries have credit cards and debt problems and stresses that may go along with them. I hope this book helps people in other countries too.

And I wish all of you dealing with credit card debt or any debt – GOOD LUCK.